I0816466

I Am Pusheen the Cat

Claire Belton

Gallery Books

New York London Toronto Sydney New Delhi

Gallery Books
An Imprint of Simon & Schuster, Inc.
1230 Avenue of the Americas
New York, NY 10020

Copyright © 2013 by Pusheen Corp.

All rights reserved, including the right to reproduce this book or portions thereof in any form whatsoever. For information, address Gallery Books Subsidiary Rights Department, 1230 Avenue of the Americas, New York, NY 10020.

This Gallery Books trade paperback edition March 2019

GALLERY BOOKS and colophon are registered trademarks of Simon & Schuster, Inc.

For information about special discounts for bulk purchases, please contact Simon & Schuster Special Sales at 1-866-506-1949 or business@simonandschuster.com.

The Simon & Schuster Speakers Bureau can bring authors to your live event. For more information or to book an event, contact the Simon & Schuster Speakers Bureau at 1-866-248-3049 or visit our website at www.simonspeakers.com.

Interior design by Joy O'Meara

Manufactured in China

35 37 39 40 38 36 34

Library of Congress Cataloging-in-Publication data is available.

ISBN 978-1-4767-4701-9
ISBN 978-1-4767-4712-5 (ebook)

For Sarah and Jake.

Special thanks to Kathleen Belton for her help preparing the illustrations for print.

Contents

Contents

Part I

I Am Pusheen the Cat

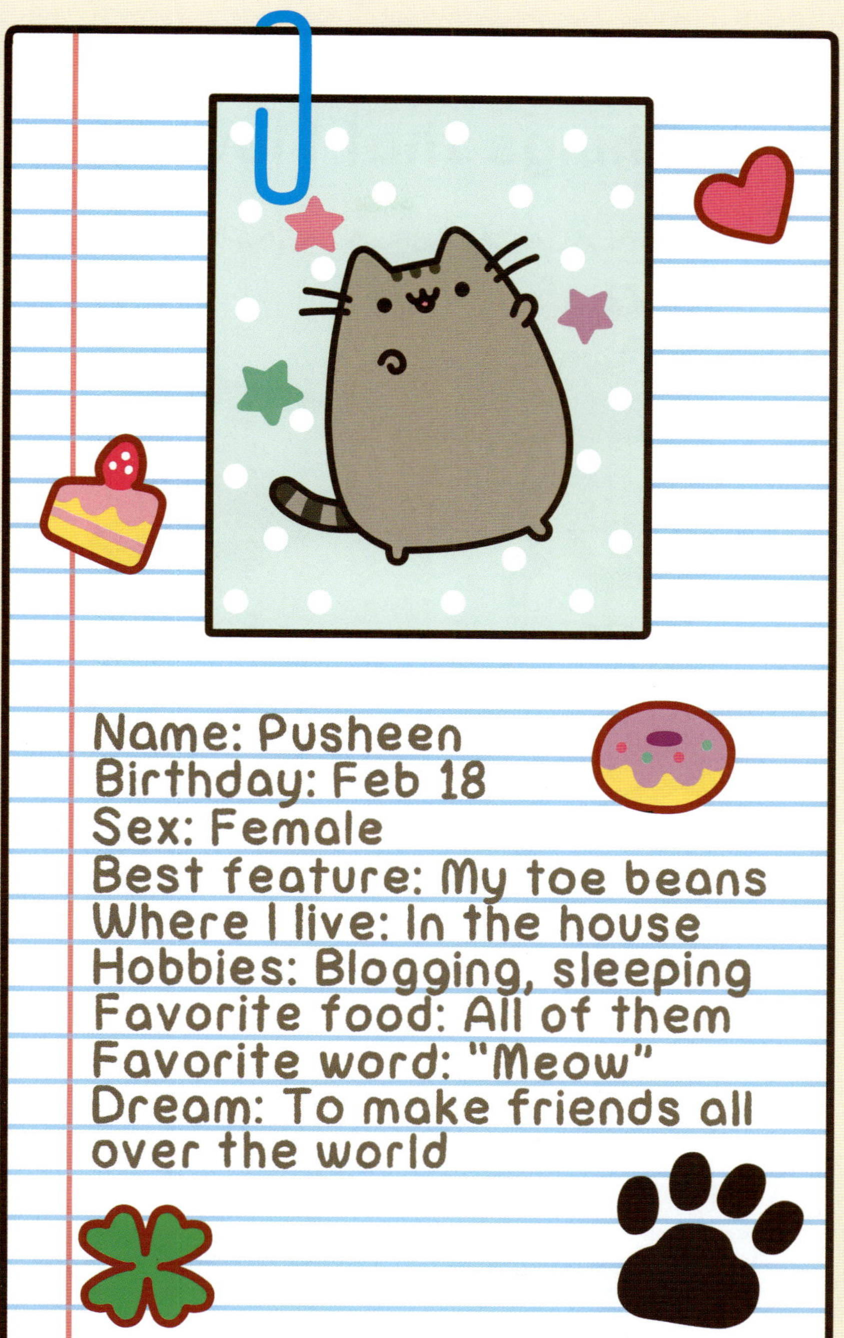
Name: Pusheen
Birthday: Feb 18
Sex: Female
Best feature: My toe beans
Where I live: In the house
Hobbies: Blogging, sleeping
Favorite food: All of them
Favorite word: "Meow"
Dream: To make friends all
over the world

Things that I love

Music

Food

Family

Sleep

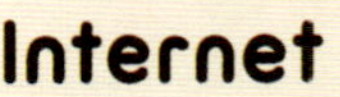

Petting chart

Yes, please!

Okay.

I will bite you.

Eat everything

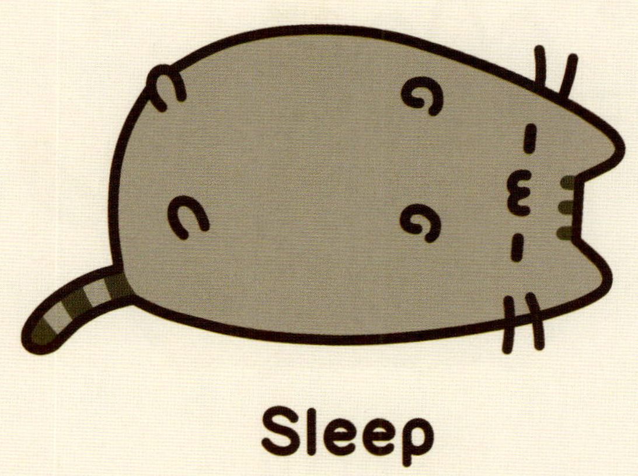

Sleep

Chill with friends

Party

Blog

My weekend plans:

Pusheen's guide to "acquiring" treats

1. Case the joint

2. Consume the target

3. Destroy the evidence

4. No remorse

Pusheen's guide to being friendly

Not friendly

Kind of friendly?

Friendly

Too friendly

Pusheen's guide to sleeping positions

The beached whale

The roast turkey

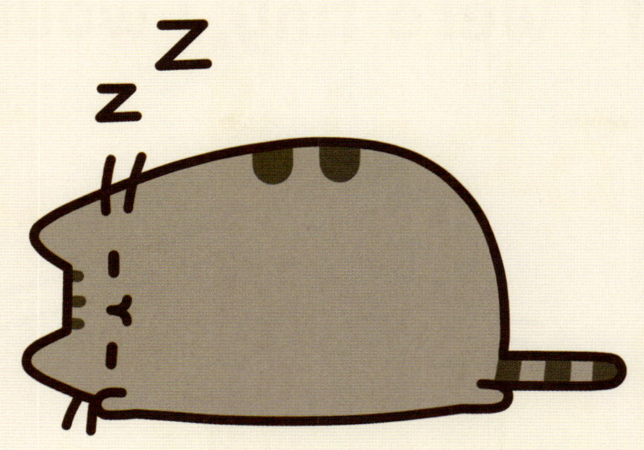

The superhero

The horizontal zombie

If I were tiny, I would...

get groomed with a toothbrush

play with thread

bathe in a teacup

sleep on a marshmallow

If cats were giant

Z
Z

Pusheen's guide to being lazy

Kind of lazy

Lazy

Very lazy

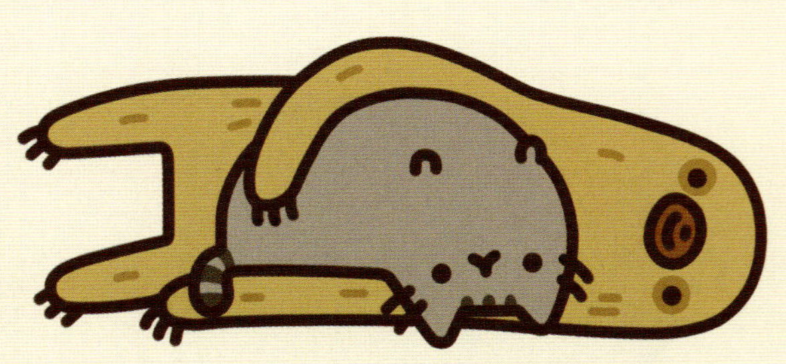

Super lazy

So lazy

can't move

5

Pusheen Games

1. Lick cold things

2. Sleep inconveniently

3. Yodeling (at 2:00 am)

4. Contortion

5. 3-meter dash

I like to drink with a straw

and pretend I'm a tiny elephant

I love snuggles

Part II

Things You Should Know About Cats

Understanding your cat's emotions

Happiness
(I've eaten recently)

Sadness
(I want more food)

Anger
(Give me more food)

Curiosity
(Where is the food?)

Contentment
(I ate all of the food)

Fear
(Will there be more?)

Things that cats kind of look like

Cat

Seal

Cat

Owl

Cat

?????

Career options for your cat

Baker

Pianist

Masseuse

Sculptor

Blogger

DJ

Things that cats apparently don't mind

Scary stories

for your cat

Once upon a time...

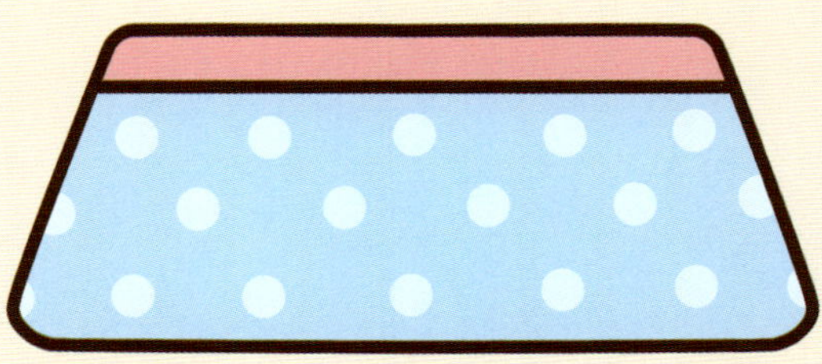

There was a food bowl.

It was empty.

The end.

Once upon a time...

There was a bathtub.

There were cats in it.

The end.

Once upon a time...

There was a vacuum cleaner.

The end.

Cat Etiquette

Remove kibbles from your dish before eating them.

If you must barf, do so on the rug.

If standing on someone, face them with your butt.

Only scratch furniture when you feel like it.

Be sure to kick litter all over the floor.

Don't forget to shed on everything!

DinoCats

Felineosaurus Rex

Stareosaurus

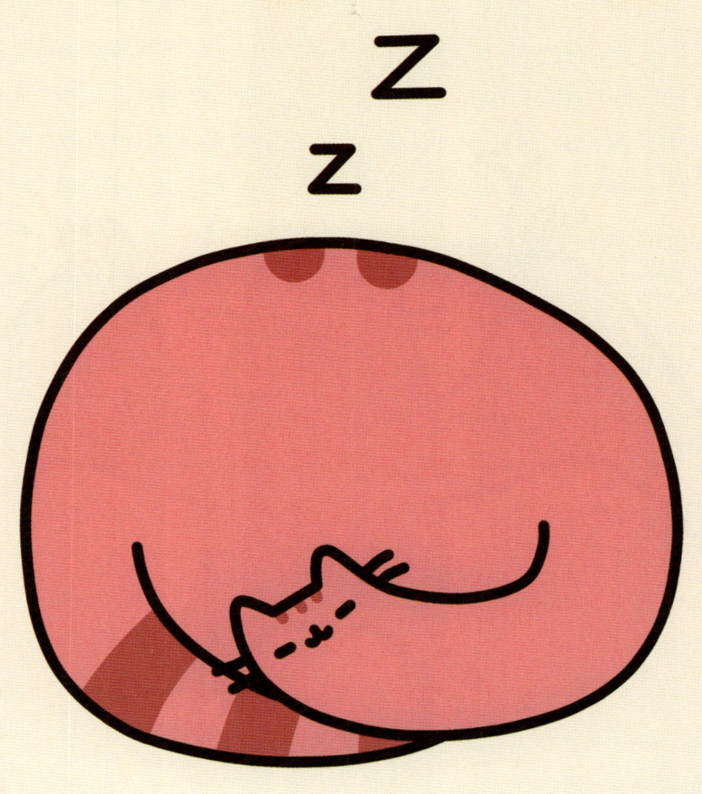

Anaposaurus

Tearodactyl

Velocicator

Playsosaurus

6 reasons you should consider being a cat

1. Free food

2. Free rent

3. Sleep as long as you want to

4. Look great with no effort

5. Toes look like beans

6. License to *kill*

Places that cats belong

The sink: No

Your shoes: No

The table: No

Your bag: No

This thing: ???

Your heart: Yes

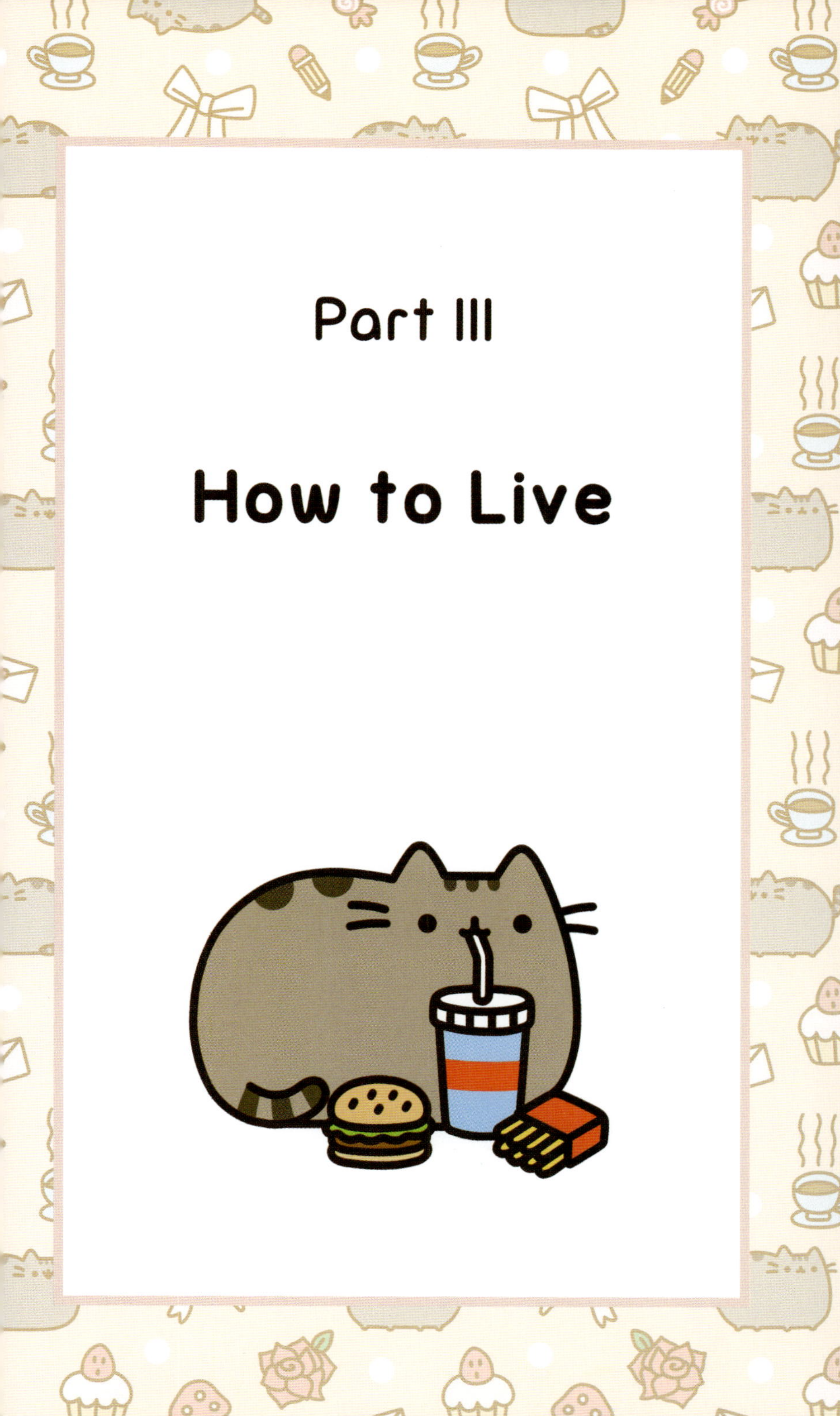

Part III

How to Live

6 practical uses for Marshmallows

1. Slippers

2. Earplugs

3. A nice hat

4. A tiny chair

5. A cool toy

6. A role model

How to tie a tie

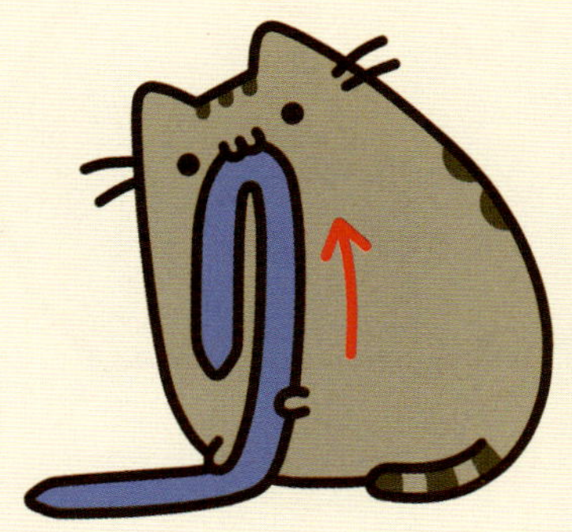

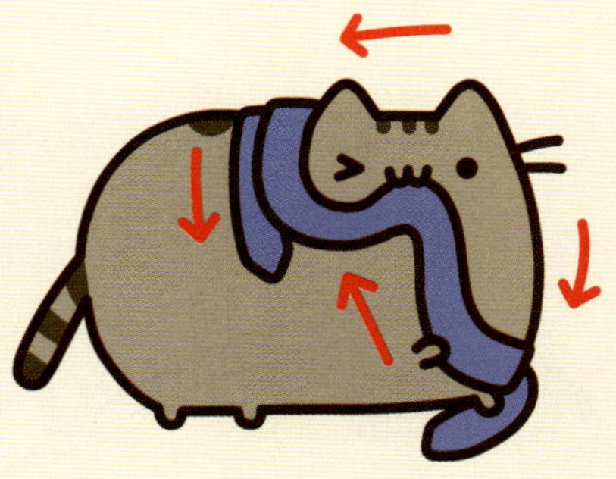

The best places to sleep

No

Yes

No

Yes

No

Yes

Pusheen's guide to being fancy

Not fancy

Kind of fancy?

Fancy

Super fancy

Fancy Pusheen

Pizza: A how-to

1. Read recipe

2. Get ingredients

3. Preheat the oven

4. Make a huge mess because you are a cat

5. Order a pizza

6. Success!!!

With tiny paws

come tiny responsibilities

Cookies:
A how-to*

1. Want cookies

2. Choose a recipe

3. Mix the stuff

4. Add candy

5. Taste the dough

6. All of it.

* Close enough

Big and

beautiful

Do-It-Yourself
Home Decor Tips
(from your cat)

DIY lace curtains

DIY chair cover

DIY shag rug

DIY floor lamp

How to have a great sleepover

1. Get makeovers

2. Watch scary movies

3. Eat junk food

4. Stay up all night

How to Procrastinate

Step 1: Ignore your work

Step 2: Have a snack

Step 3: Take a nap

Step 4: Forget what you were doing

Tech support tips

from your cat

Have you tried chewing on it?*

* Please don't

How about headbutting it?

Have you tried knocking it off of the desk?

How about staring at it?

Not helping?

Better sleep on it.

Pusheen's vacation to Japan

Part IV

Stormy

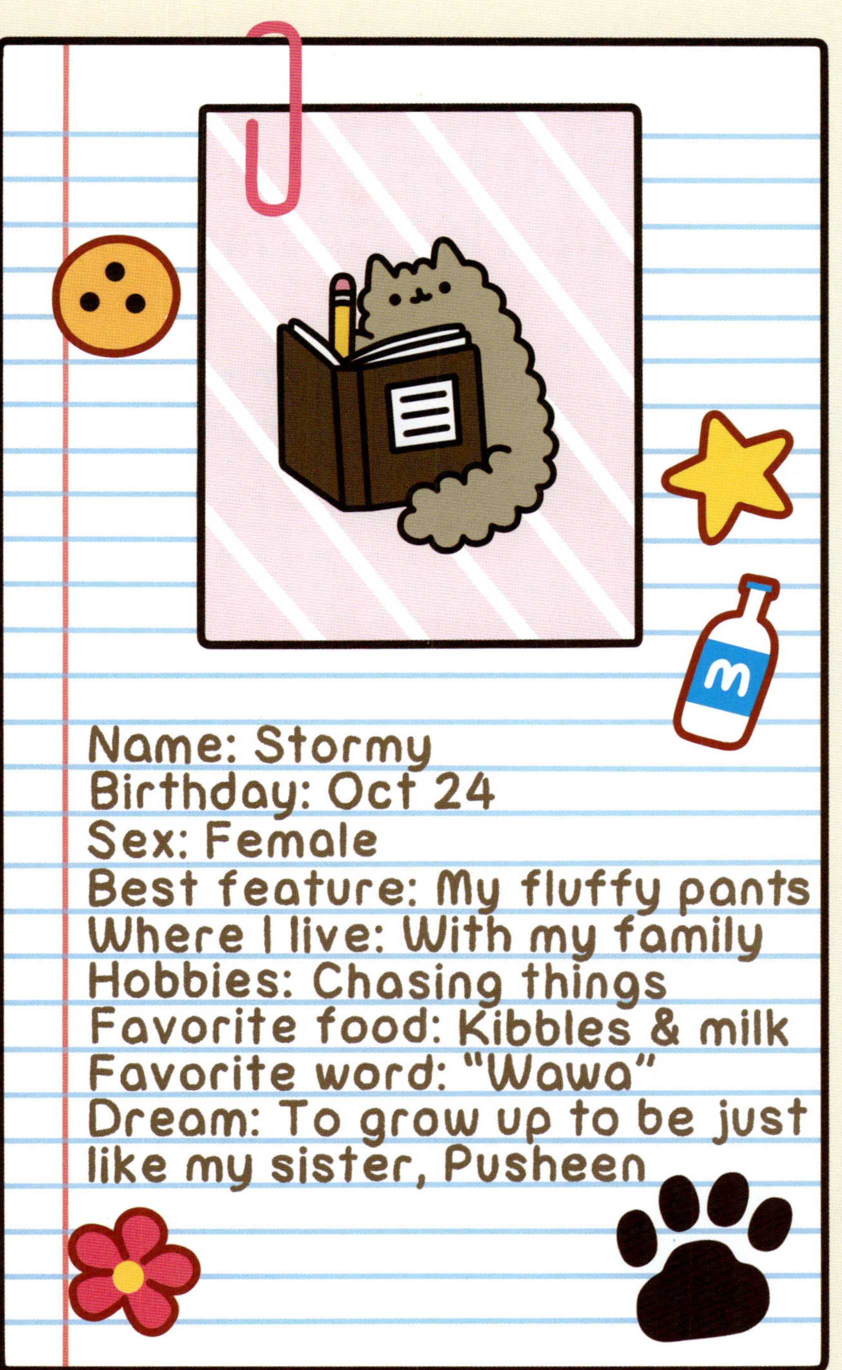
Name: Stormy
Birthday: Oct 24
Sex: Female
Best feature: My fluffy pants
Where I live: With my family
Hobbies: Chasing things
Favorite food: Kibbles & milk
Favorite word: "Wawa"
Dream: To grow up to be just like my sister, Pusheen

The joys of having a younger sibling (starring Stormy)

Mom says to share!

Wasn't us.

Friends forever.

Kitten Adventures
with Stormy the Cat

The adventure

The reality

The adventure

The reality

The adventure

The reality

Stormy's guide to sleeping positions

The accordion

The storm cloud

The piggyback

Box size guide

The single

The double

The queen

The king

The princess

Cat Wizards

Which superpower would you choose?

1. Flight

2. Invisibility

3. Mind reading

4. Telekinesis

5. Super strength

6. Breathe underwater

Part V

A Year in the Life of Pusheen

Three...

Two...

One...

HAPPY NEW YEAR!

New Year's resolutions

Expectation

Reality

Expectation

Reality

Valentines from your cat

???

Sorry
not
sorry

1. Have breakfast

2. Food coma

3. Wear green

Puisín (Pusheen) means "kitten"

4. Study Irish

5. Get lucky

Wake me up in spring

Reasons I love spring

Warm weather

Easter

April showers

May flowers

Picnics

~~Bugs~~

Spring-cleaning guide

1. Clean the dishes

2. Clean out the fridge

3. Put away your toys

4. Prune the houseplants

5. Do the laundry

6. Dust everything

Expectation

Reality

Expectation

Reality

Expectation

Reality

How to celebrate on the

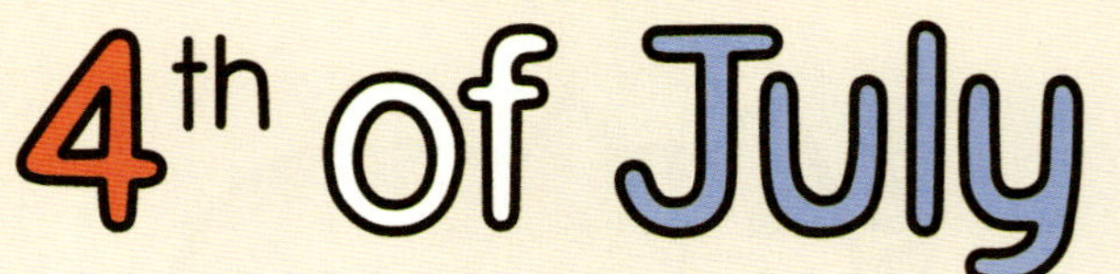

1. Dress appropriately

2. Eat some BBQ

3. Think about eagles and stuff

4. Watch fireworks

My beach essentials

Donuts

Cake

Pizza

Bacon

Too hot.

Need ice cream.

Reasons I love fall

1. Pie

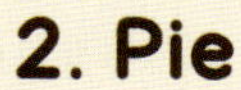

2. Pie

3. Pie

4. Pie

5. Pie

6. Also pie

BOO!

Lazy costume ideas (for your cat)

A mummy

A ghost

A box

A witch

A superhero

A monster

No-shave November styling suggestions

The dad-stache

The scarf-stache

The Santa

The eyebrows

The elegante

~~The butt-stache~~
not recommended

The Pusheen way

1. Eat turkey

2. Eat pie

3. Eat turkey and pie

4. Take a nap

5. Wake up & repeat from step 1

5-second rule

How to make the best snowman

1. Make a body

2. Add eyes

3. Add a smile

4. Add a nose

5. Add sprinkles

6. Enjoy!

Things your cat wants for Christmas

✗ No

✓ Yes

No

Yes

Christmas

to-do list

☑ Decorate the tree

Wrap the gifts

Make cookies ~~for Santa~~

mrowrooomyao

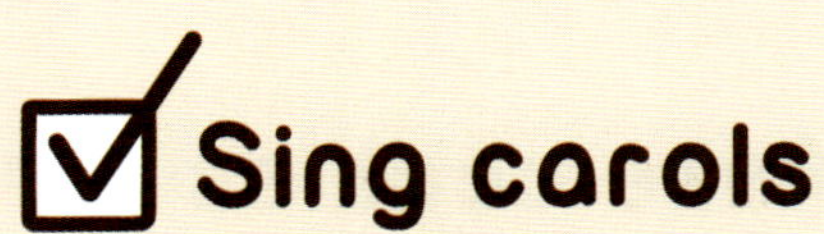

☑ Spend time with family

DEC

Wait for Santa

How to catch Santa

1. Set your bait

2. Wait

3. Don't eat the bait

4. Don't do it

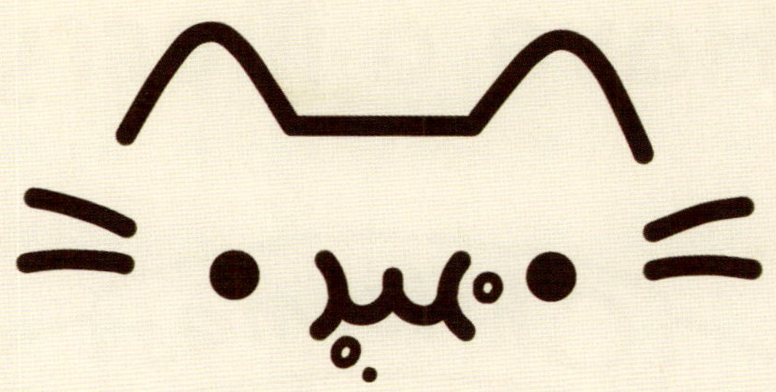

5. Stop!!

6. You ruined it

Have a Merry

For More Pusheen, Find Her Online

www.pusheen.com

Instagram: @pusheen

Facebook: @pusheen

Twitter: @pusheen

About the Author

Claire Belton is an artist and entrepreneur based in Chicago. She spends her time petting cats, drawing cats, and pursuing cat-related endeavors.

About Pusheen

Pusheen is a chubby tabby cat that Claire's family adopted from a shelter when she was a kitten. She enjoys snuggling, grooming herself, and generally being adorable.

Home

is where my butt is.

Discover more from Pusheen!

And the mini edition!

Available wherever books are sold or
at SimonandSchuster.com